A New True Book

THE TLINGIT

By Alice Osinski

CHILDREN'S PRESS
A Division of Grolier Publishing
Sherman Turnpike
Danbury, Connecticut 06816

PHOTO CREDITS

Photographs Courtesy Alaska State Library—Winter & Pond Collection—12 (left #PCA 87-237 and right #PCA 87-182), 13 (left #PCA 87-244 and right #PCA 87-35), 14 (#PCA 87-333,c.1), 20 (#PCA 87-64), 21 (#PCA 87-106), 22 (left #PCA 87-176), 23 (left #PCA 87-39,c.1), 31 (#PCA 87-65), 38 (#PCA 87-334), 39 (top left #PCA 87-242 and bottom left #PCA 87-326 and right #PCA 87-139), 44 (left #PCA 87-200 and right #PCA 87-7)

© Reinhard Brucker—22 (right), 24 (4 photos), 35 (2 photos)

Joan Dunlop—8 (right), 32, 41

Virginia Grimes—6 (bottom)

Reprinted with permission of *The New Book of Knowledge*, 1989 edition, © Grolier Inc.—5

Historical Pictures Service, Chicago—37

Museum of the American Indian—26 (bottom right #4611), 36 (right #4222)

R/C Photo Agency—© J.M. Halama, 10 (bottom), 16 (2 photos)

Chris Roberts Represents—© Slocomb, 2

Shostal Associates/SuperStock International, Inc.—8 (bottom left); © Ernest Manewal, 19 (top right), 23 (right)

Bob & Ira Spring—Cover, 6 (top), 7, 10 (top), 15, 17, 19 (left and bottom right), 26 (left and top right), 27, 29 (2 photos), 33, 36 (left), 40 (2 photos), 42, 43 (2 photos), 45

Tom Stack & Associates—© Leonard Lee Rue III, 8 (top left); © Jeff Foott, 9

COVER: Chilkat dancers use historic Chilkat blankets in authentic tribal house.

For Tlingit children who continue to dream their ancestors' dreams

Library of Congress Cataloging-in-Publication Data

Osinski, Alice.
    The Tlingit / by Alice Osinski.
      p.   cm. — (A New true book)
    Includes index.
    Summary: Describes the traditional life-style, arts and crafts, changing land, and modern life of the Tlingit Indians.
      ISBN 0-516-01189-8
      1. Tlingit Indians—Juvenile literature. [1. Tlingit Indians. 2. Indians of North America.] I. Title.
E99.T6085   1990   89-25345
973'.04972—dc20   CIP
                                                AC

TABLE OF CONTENTS

COMING TO ALASKA

Along the southeast coast of Alaska a group of Native Americans have been fishing for thousands of years. They call themselves the Tlingit (pronounced *klink-it*).

Ancestors of the Tlingit came to Alaska thousands of years ago, when much of the land was covered by large sheets of ice called glaciers. Today, Tlingit

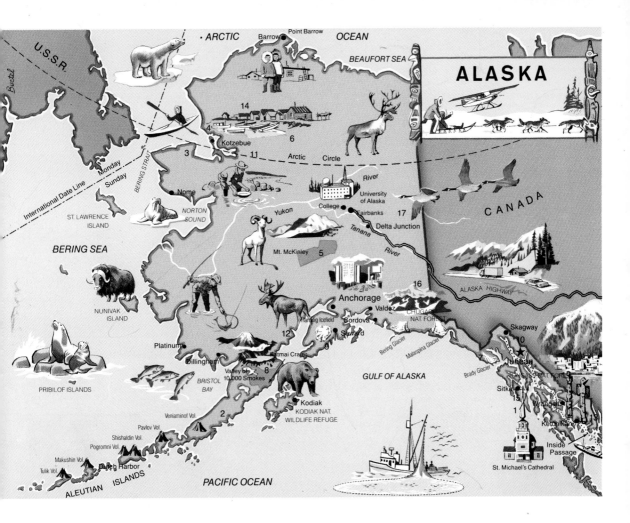

people live in many
communities in Southeast
Alaska. The society is
divided into two groups
called Raven and Eagle.

5

Alaska has thick cedar forests (below) and beautiful sunsets (above).

A LAND OF PLENTY

Southeastern Alaska is a good place to live. It has a mild climate year-round. There are plenty of animals to hunt, fish to catch, and berries to eat. The nearby forests provide wood for fuel and for building houses.

The village of Hoonah, Alaska

Salmon (top left) swimming upstream. Salmon can be dried in the sun (bottom left), or grilled over a fire (above).

Fish, especially salmon, is a main source of food for the Tlingit. Salmon can be eaten fresh or dried. Often, it is cooked over a smoking fire

to give it a special flavor.

In the past, the Tlingit set up fishing camps in the spring and fall. They speared the salmon as they swam upstream, or caught them in nets or traps. Today, the Tlingit use fishing boats to catch salmon with seine nets and gill nets. Sometimes

A woman netting fish (left)

Small canneries like the one above prepare fish for market. Right, a man bones a halibut.

they use fishing poles. Many
Tlingit sell their catch to
big companies.

In addition to salmon, the
Tlingit catch halibut, herring,
cod, and crabs. Along some
rivers, fish called euchalon
(candlefish) are gathered in
nets. A tasty oil comes from
the euchalon. Some people
like to dip their food in
this oil.

The old man and child wear clothing made from goat hair, animal furs, and bird feathers.

In the past, hunting was very important to the Tlingit. They hunted sea lions and otters along the rocky shores. Those who lived inland hunted mountain goats, bear, and deer. From

Items that Tlingits wear or carry identify them as members of a certain clan.

these animals, they fed and clothed their families. Because hunting was such dangerous and necessary work, good hunters were respected.

VILLAGE LIFE

The ancestors of today's
Tlingit people lived very
busy lives. In the summer
and fall of each year, they
set up temporary fishing
camps to gather food. Then,
before winter set in, they

Chief Shakes's tribal home is on a tiny island in the inner harbor of Wrangell.

returned to their villages. There, several families lived together in large houses made of cedar.

The houses were painted with colorful pictures of animals and birds. Sometimes, the Tlingit made carvings

15

Tlingit homes painted
with colorful designs

of animals on the wooden
posts that supported the
houses, or on the doorways
and entrances. Tall wooden
carvings, called totem poles,
stood in front of the houses.
Some totem poles were
twenty feet high. They were
carved with brightly painted

Chief Kadashan totem poles on Shakes Island

figures that represented a family, a clan, birds, or animals. Totem poles recorded family and clan history.

After a totem pole was raised, a ceremony was held. Someone would tell the story of the carved figures on the pole and explain why they were placed in a particular order.

In many Tlingit communities

Family and clan histories are
recorded on totem poles.

today, you can see
beautifully carved cedar
houses and totem poles.

BASKET WEAVING AND WOOD CARVING

During the cold, rainy months of winter, Tlingit families wove blankets, mats, and baskets. They also carved beautiful wooden boxes, tools, and masks.

These basket weavers in Sitka, Alaska, were photographed in 1897.

The Tlingit were very skillful at making containers from the fibers of grasses and the roots of plants. First they soaked the fibers in water to soften them. Then the women skillfully wove the fibers into baskets. Some baskets were used to carry

things or for storage.
Others were woven so tightly that
they were waterproof.
These were used for cooking.
   Mats woven from strips of
cedar bark had several uses.
Some were used in women's
clothing, or as bedding.

Large mats were hung from
the ceiling to separate
different living areas.

Women wove blankets
from goat wool and
cedar bark. The designs
were created by the men.

Designs on many blankets
and robes represented the
bear, the whale, or the raven.

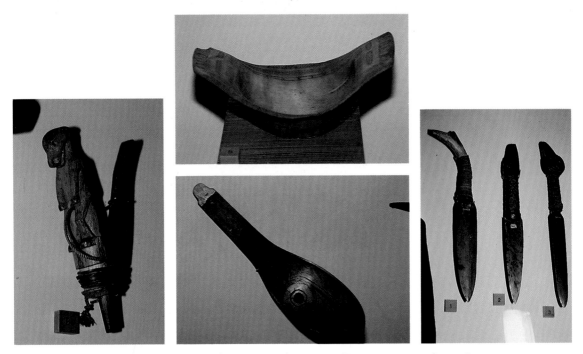

The carved fishhook (left), bowl (top center), spoon (bottom center), and knives (far right), were a necessary part of daily life.

Boxes made from cedarwood were used for cooking and for storing food and household items. They were beautifully carved and painted. The Tlingit also carved and painted their dishes, tools, weapons, and fishhooks.

STORYTELLING

During the winter, the
Tlingit also spent time
recalling the important
events of the past year. They
did not write down their
history. Instead, they used
storytelling and plays that
included dancing to pass
down their history and their
values to their children. Most
dancers were dressed as
creatures of the sea and the
forest, especially the raven,

Dancers wear clothing, masks, and headdresses that represent the animals they imitate, such as the raven (top right) and killer whale (above right). Chief Kat-Lean wore the raven headdress during a fight he had in 1802 with the Russians at Old Fort Sitka.

the bear, and the killer whale. While a drummer beat his drum, the dancers would imitate the movements of the animals. A certain combination of movements

told a particular story. As they danced, singers or storytellers told the stories.

Today, the Tlingit still perform these dances and tell the same stories their ancestors told so long ago.

GIFT GIVING

The biggest event of the
winter for the Tlingit was
a feast called a potlatch.
Sometimes it lasted four
days or more. Families gave
these feasts to mark an
important event in their lives
such as the birth or death of
a family member, or some
special achievement. During
a potlatch, there was much
dancing, storytelling, and gift
giving. The gifts included
food, blankets, canoes, and

People celebrate the raising
of a totem pole.

even fishing rights. The
number of gifts showed how
generous the families were
and how important the event
was to them. In most Tlingit
communities today, potlatches
still take place.

CARVING A CANOE

The Tlingit have always made their living from the sea. Those who lived a long time ago hunted and fished from small canoes. Large canoes took them on long trading trips, to special feasts, or to war. Often, they traveled great distances to trade with other people. Among the items they traded were fish oil, shells, copper, furs, carvings, and woven blankets.

Building a canoe was a
special event in the village.
Although many people
helped to make the canoe, a
master carver was in charge.
He chose the men who went
into the forest to chop down
the red or yellow cedar tree.

Design on a Tlingit canoe

Then he watched over all the stages of building the canoe.

After the tree was hollowed out, it was carried to the water's edge. There it was carefully carved and shaped so that it would handle easily and move smoothly through the water.

Finally, it was given a name and painted with family emblems, or crests.

Today, the Tlingit still build colorfully carved canoes, but most Tlingit families fish in large modern boats that have motors.

RELIGION

Tlingits have always been closely tied to nature. Their beliefs have centered on the Creator of Life and on spirit helpers who have power to influence such things as weather, hunting, and healing the sick.

Shamans wore masks during certain ceremonies.

In traditional Tlingit society, special people, called shamans, would contact spirit helpers for guidance.

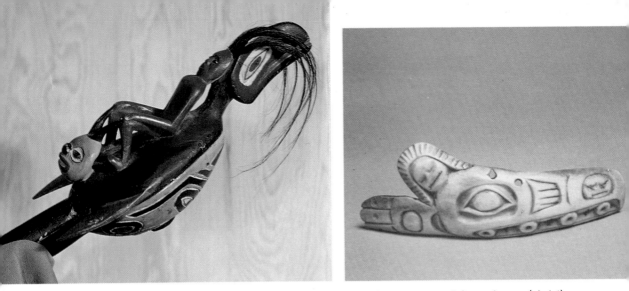

A wooden rattle (left) and a shaman's eagle-head charm carved from ivory (right)

During certain ceremonies, shamans would wear special masks and robes. They would sing songs and request favors from the spirit helpers.

Today, many Tlingit communities are Christian. Yet, traditional beliefs still influence their lives.

Vitus Bering

THE CHANGING LAND

In the 1700s, Vitus Bering, a Danish explorer working for the czar of Russia, came to Alaska. He claimed all the land for Russia. Before long, Russian fur traders began building forts and setting up trading companies. They took the land away from the Tlingit.

The Treadwell gold mine in 1899

The Tlingit fought bravely
to keep their land. Many died
in battle. In 1867, Russia sold
Alaska to the United States.
In the 1870s, gold was discovered
in southeast Alaska. Soon
thousands of people came

to mine the gold and live in Alaska. Missionaries built churches and schools. The United States government began to build schools, too. All these events changed the Tlingit way of life.

These pictures show how Tlingit clothing changed after the Tlingit were ruled by outsiders.

Tlingit elders continue to teach the
history and customs of their people.

MODERN LIFE

Today, the Tlingit people have a modern life-style, but the old ways are mixed with the new. Many Tlingit still live in small villages and towns along the coast. They live by logging, fishing, and hunting. Others own

Sitka, Alaska

The harbor of Sitka

businesses in large cities
such as Sitka and Juneau.
Many work as artists,
teachers, lawyers, and
priests, and many work for
the government.

Today, modern Tlingit artists (below) continue to carve the magnificent totem poles that their ancestors carved in prehistoric times (left).

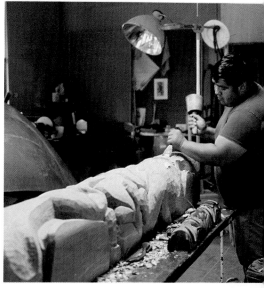

But whether the Tlingit live in cities or in villages, they try to preserve the customs and traditions of the past.

Tlingit dancers in the early 1900s

Long ago, ancestors of the modern Tlingit fought to keep their land and their customs. Today, as Americans, the Tlingit are still struggling to preserve them. They are working together to pass laws to protect the land and their right to use it. They are

sending their children to
schools that will prepare
them for the future while
their elders work to preserve
the beauty of their past.

WORDS YOU SHOULD KNOW

Bering, Vitus (BAIR • ing VHY • tus) — Danish navigator who first sighted Alaska in 1741

cedar (SEE • der) — a tall tree of the pine family, noted for its fragrant wood

clan (KLAN) — a group of families with a common ancestor

climate (KLY • mit) — the average weather of a place over a period of years

crest (KRESST) — an emblem representing a family or other group

emblem (EM • blem) — a picture symbolizing a group or an idea

feast (FEEST) — a meal celebrating a special event

gill nets (GILL NEHTS) — flat fishing nets that hang vertically in the water

glacier (GLAY • sher) — a large body of ice covering a land surface

halibut (HAL • uh • but) — a large flatfish

herring (HAIR • ing) — a small food fish

Juneau (JOO • no) — a city and port in southeastern Alaska

otter (AH • ter) — a fish-eating mammal

potlatch (PAHT • latch) — a feast marked by the giving of gifts

preserve (pri • ZERV) — to keep

Russia (RUH • shuh) — a former empire in northern Europe and Asia

seine nets (SAYN NEHTS) — large, vertical nets used to enclose fish when the ends are pulled together

shaman (SHAH • min) — a person who is believed to have contact with the spirit world and who is skilled in curing diseases

temporary (TEM • puh • rayr • ee) — for a limited time
Tlingit (KLINK • it) — American Indians who live in southeastern Alaska
totem pole (TOH • tem POHL) — a pole carved or painted with symbols that represent a family history

INDEX

About the Author

Alice Osinski launched her career in writing after teaching Native American children for seven years in Pine Ridge, South Dakota, and Gallup, New Mexico. She has developed bicultural curricula for alternative school programs in South Dakota and New Mexico. Her articles and children's stories have appeared in textbooks for D.C. Heath and Open Court. She has written several books for Childrens Press in the New True Book series, including The Sioux, The Chippewa, The Eskimo, The Navajo, *and* The Nez Perce.